Seed of a Servant

Heavenlygift Hearthstones

Published by Heavenlygift Hearthstones, 2024.

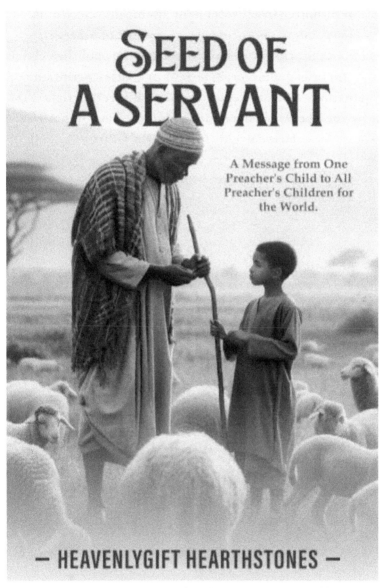

Copyright 2024 by Heavenlygift Hearthstones. All rights reserved. This book is protected by copyright. No part of this book may be reproduced, stored in a retrieval system, or transmitted in any form or by any means - electronic, mechanical, photocopying, recording, or otherwise - without the prior written permission of the publisher, except for brief quotations in reviews or articles. Scripture quotations are from Legacy Standard Bible, copyright 2021 by The Lockman Foundation . Published in South Africa. Heavenlygift Hearthstones © 2024

While every precaution has been taken in the preparation of this book, the publisher assumes no responsibility for errors or omissions, or for damages resulting from the use of the information contained herein.

SEED OF A SERVANT

First edition. December 20, 2024.

Copyright © 2024 Heavenlygift Hearthstones.

ISBN: 979-8224185153

Written by Heavenlygift Hearthstones.

Also by Heavenlygift Hearthstones

Hate in the dark
Seed of a Servant

Dedicated to my parents, my siblings and other Preacher's children

Contents

- Dedication

- Foreword

- Introduction

- Common Misconceptions

- Your parents' salvation is not your inheritance.

- We're also called from birth

- Prioritizing Prayer

- Unlearning the wrong kinds of teachings

- Having the heart of discipline

- Asking Questions is allowed

- Healing is an art

- You are not raised by the church

- Living your life giving God all the Glory

- Five main things I learnt from my father that I couldn't learn anywhere else

Epilogue

DEDICATION

Not a single word of this book would have been possible if it wasn't for the obedience of my parents to accept the Calling from God into their lives and to remain resilient in their calling through a multitude of challenges they remained faithful to where God has called them.

Thank you so much Ps O. Hearthstones and T.M. Hearthstones

Foreword

In this world we live in there are people who have been called by God to serve in His field. By being obedient to this calling they surrender every plan they had about the future in this world. They follow Jesus full-time (Matthew 4:17-22). If married, their families get to know a new life.

The wife is expected to help her husband in this calling. Their children also have no choice, they have to help somehow in whatever their father is doing. Sometimes or most of the time servants of God are treated in a bad way, either by members of the local church or by seniors of the church, regionally or nationally. This can have a negative impact on children. It's unfortunate. Repentance is needed

Ps O Hearthstones

Introduction

Being born into a family of a minister, it has always intrigued me as to why was I born into this family, God chose a family of a Pastor for me and all along I never truly understood the amount of responsibility I had in writing this book as I did on this one Wednesday evening when God put it in my heart to write this book.

At first I thought I would write an answer book where I'll be sure to clarify quite a few realities of being a Pastor's Child but then I realized that the one thing I've always needed as a child, growing up was a book by the child of a Servant about the truths I need to realize about myself as I'm in the position I was born into.

It wasn't by accident nor was it by chance that I was born here, I was born into this family for a specific purpose which I am living out each and every day. I was graced into this life that I live which I would never trade for anything which is the very fabric of who I am, I am proud to say that I am the son of a preacher and in life I've learnt so many lessons some of which I'm still learning and even some which I am yet to learn.

Chapter One

Common Misconceptions

When you meet someone and they tell you that they do a particular job such as they're a police officer, the first thing that happens naturally in your mind is you imagine them chasing down a criminal, catching them and arresting them. Well what would you think if when you had to ask them a question such as "how many people have you arrested so far?" they answer you and say that they've never arrested a single person in their three year career? It would be a surprise right? Well here is the thing about anyone you'll meet, they are naturally going to make assumptions about you the same way you'll make assumptions about them. We're hardwired to make assumptions in any scenario before we actually get the full story.

However, sometimes people tend to hold on to these assumptions until they turn them into misconceptions. Misconceptions are when someone actually believes what they assume to be true and it's always very hard to make them believe otherwise. I have met so many people in my life and many of them have had their own misconceptions about my life and now I don't even bother myself by trying to explain how they're wrong about who we are as preacher's children.

We are only humans like everyone else in the world, the only difference being that we're born on what most can say a pedestal, it is very similar to being born into royalty where we're born with all eyes on us as to what will we do with our lives within the church and how will we act even outside of the church.

It is very normal for people who are born with a surname of someone who is well known to meet people and people have an assumption about their lives and that can be good because that means our parents have a legacy but a legacy sometimes can be a bad legacy which then makes you sharing your name and blood with someone who is known and not in a good way but a bad way but those who are born into a good legacy even for them it can be good or bad because you born and people can be expecting you to follow in the footsteps of your parents and if you do follow in their footsteps they will be watching closely to see any similarity or difference in the way you are carrying on in the legacy. It can also be bad in the sense that if you fully don't follow your parents footsteps then you are being rebellious simply for choosing your own legacy to start.

You won't be a preacher since your father is a preacher
This is the most common misconception in the world. Everyone I've met in my life and heart that my father is a pastor has said to me that me and my siblings will be wild due to the fact that our father is a pastor. This can be true and this is because one thing of having your father as a pastor (shephard) it means that he will be tending to other people's needs while almost forgetting his family and I've seen it in other families however my father had a beautiful balance of family and the church, we never for a single moment felt abandoned by him at all.

In other case this may be true in the sense that us as the children of ministers get to see behind the scenes and see things which can misconstrue our perception of what Christianity is based on how a church has treated our parents because the reality is that there is no church in this world that is fully perfect every church has a lot of flaws and that is fine because Jesus didn't die for perfect people and even Christians can be flawed sometimes and through that we then start to question and doubt what Christianity truly is and through that we then start to act out and experiment on other things which may be other religions and beliefs or sometimes just go into worldly things.

This can be true because God does call us all into different things so it is normal for a preacher's child to not be a preacher himself because God may have called him into a different ministry such as music, writing, acting etc... Parents should never pressure their children into being preachers because those who are not called into ministry may actually lead people astray simply because they are doing what their parents are calling them to and not what God has truly called them to. We are all playing little parts in what God is doing in the world so we all can't do the same thing or have the same function (1 Corinthians 12:12-31). The church and God's plan for the world would easily fail because of the fact that we are all doing the same thing.

You live a perfect Christian life
One of the funniest parts of having been in a preacher's family has been whenever there would be a guest who comes to stay with us for a few days or a few weeks has been them being surprised firstly with our huge love and passion for sports especially if they come during the weekend they'll see us watching football then an hour or so later watching cricket and

out of nowhere watch rugby and then hear us having conversations about more sports like formula 1, basketball and more and then whenever there would be a goal, try, wicket or see someone we're rooting for win and we just jump off the couch and celebrate on the top of our lungs while clapping. They would also get surprised with our choice of favorite horror movies, and hear us listening to any and every style of music. Then whenever they were about to leave they would always say the famous phrase "Your family really surprised me but I like the way you are".

My family always surprises many people and even other preacher's children can relate to most of what I wrote there. In my family the best thing my parents did for us as children was to allow us to be fully ourselves and at the same time teach us how to have our own devotional time and prayer time during the day and then in the evening we're praying as a family which is where our father would give us some nuggets of wisdom when it comes to the Bible, or quiz us on our biblical knowledge. It's also where he teaches us about basic human things concerning the world we're living in. I fully believe that it was through that kind of foundation that me and all my siblings have a wonderful relationship with God. We could easily be elsewhere but it was through our parents' prayers over us and them giving us the freedom that we're here close as siblings and rather hang out with each other than to hang out with other people.

No we don't know the Bible through and through, we have passages memorized but that doesn't mean we know the Bible fully as we know ourselves. We enjoy reading the Bible and reading other Christian books because they are the ones that perfect our Christian walk.

Even our prayer life is going to be different than one might think, each person's prayer life is always different so you won't find us praying like our parents' prayers which you hear in church.

The biggest guarantee I can give you about our Christian lives is that they are not perfect. We also sin and sometimes we can get caught in a situation where we are living in sin but the seed of being in a church through our childhood works as a seed as to our lives as adults because we get to go back and repent and get forgiveness of our sins and Jesus moves into our hearts.

We are the first to hear the revelation/sermon our fathers have

There are moments where our father will tell us a revelation before other people may know about it but even then it would be when he is preaching here at home but in most cases we would only hear the revelation with other people who aren't in the family. When one gets a revelation, God will also instruct them as to when and where to share it. It does happen that someone has received a revelation but only speaks it after years and that's because God's timing is always the best timing and God knows when the revelation will land on the soil that's ready to yield fruit.

We truly never hear any sermon before other people because my father doesn't believe in repeating a sermon unless it is necessary to do so and when God instructs him to do so. So he does tell us that he already knows what he will teach/preach when he has a talking engagement but he wouldn't tell us what it's about even if we won't be there and we'll probably only know about it either through someone who heard him speak or if God instructs him to repeat it to us. At the end of the day everything goes back to what God is leading him to and him being obedient to it.

The reality is that the whole thought of that because someone is born into a certain kind of family then they're so and so is completely wrong because in reality 90% of what you think about them is wrong and even anyone who is just living a normal life, if you will make any sort of assumption about their life then you are jumping to wrong conclusions because the best thing you can do for anyone is to hear their story and to fully hear it and not even try to understand them on your own strength but give them a chance to help you understand them. We are all human being created uniquely and beautiful and the only way to truly love someone is to listen to them, study them, see them because most of the conflict is based on people misunderstanding each other and to speak out any assumption or misconception to them in some cases you may be speaking it and they will end up acting out what you spoke because we need to remember that through our words we create things and the tongue is a very powerful instrument let's try to us it for the good things only and to speak positivity only.

James 3:5
In the same way, the tongue is a small thing that makes grand speeches. But a tiny spark can set a great forest on fire.

Chapter two

Your Parents' salvation is not your inheritance

On the 7th of April 2007, an alter call was made for children, it was a rainy Saturday afternoon in the church I attended Good Friday in, I lifted my hands and went forward to accept Jesus into my heart that day, 10 years later in the same church I accepted Jesus, I got baptized on a Saturday once again. This is one of the few times I shared my salvation story and when I got baptized. The man that led me in the salvation prayer was not my father and the other man that baptized me was not my father at all, my father has been the one who has had a front row seat in my Christian journey. However, he has ensured that he teaches me the same things he taught anyone else, he corrected me where I needed correction and reprimanded me when I strayed.

Myself and my siblings have had a pleasure of having parents who never tried to walk the walk of a relationship with Christ for us, they taught us His ways but they never forced us to do something because we're their children, instead they allowed the Holy Spirit to work in us and bring about the change in our lives that we truly need. We made many mistakes along the way but they made us have our own relationship with Jesus and be more dependent on Him than we are to our parents.

It would be so easy to assume that a gracious God would give a free pass into heaven to anyone who comes from the lineage of a preacher, yet that's not the case, in fact when you think about it, it is so much better to have your own relationship with God because the reward you find in Heaven is incredible and you know it was worth it. In Proverbs 13:11 you find the scripture talking about how when you obtain money easily you lose it very fast, and that's because you don't appreciate it like the person who would appreciate it more because they obtained it from working hard and now know that it was all worth it. Luckily, our walk with Jesus is not about hard work at all, it is the most simple thing one can get, it's through just believing in the finished work of Jesus Christ at the cross.

It all begins in our real belief of Jesus and His work at the Cross and that He is in heaven waiting for us to join Him there. We were born into a world that is filled with sin and unending evil. We unfortunately are born sinners ourselves regardless of who our parents are, they are there only as our parents, the conduits that have given us earthly life and the ones who are there to teach us how to walk, talk and live our lives in the way that God leads them to do so. That then means that us, as their children will come to a point in our lives where we have to make a choice between Jesus and what the outside world can offer, we may know the entire Bible by memory but with the way Jesus chases us down in our sin, one day we'll realize that we know absolutely nothing about Christianity and just the magnitude of God's love for us.

In most cases you'd actually find the fact that someone ends up leaving Christianity as a whole due to the fact that his/her parents were badly mistreated. The reality is that we get exposed fully to the church from both sides of the fence, the good side of the church and unfortunately the bad side. It's the reality that there is no such thing as a perfect church because it is run by and full of imperfect human beings who can easily hurt other human beings and the one thing they don't realize is the fact that the children get the ramifications of their actions and the children actually get to see their parents having to come to grips of the hurt they experienced in the church they once worked in. Sometimes it may not always be someone hurting their parents but just the children actually seeing the hypocrisy of some people who on a Sunday come acting holier than thou yet the children know their shortfallings.

In other cases yet again, you might find that some children are in a place where they are wrestling a few things with God and think that because their friends get to enjoy the worldly life they are happier than them, they will find themselves taking a detour into the world to try finding this happiness they see all around them. It is the biggest weapon the enemy uses against you, you might think that you are missing out on so much and yet you will realize the amount of emptiness people hide behind the smiles when they are in these places that give you temporary happiness, yet with God you find eternal joy that nobody can take away through His Word and also His presence in your life.

I now can't imagine life without God and many people have wondered how am I a Christian and I can say that it's through my parents showing me the Word of God in what they always taught me and even their lives, my parents lived Deuteronomy 6:7 and raised us through it and it's not because they were perfect Christians but it was simply because they were honest with us about God and taught us His Word and encouraged us to read it for ourselves and allowed us to have an impact of God in our lives to have the revelation of who He truly is and now I live to serve Him day in and day out because I know that He is truly real and ever present.

Chapter Three

We're also called from birth

Exodus 31:1-11

"And Yahweh spoke to Moses, saying, "See, I have called by name Bezalel, the son of Uri, the son of Hur, of the tribe of Judah. And I have filled him with the Spirit of God in wisdom, in discernment, in knowledge, and in all kinds of craftsmanship, to devise artistic designs for work in gold, in silver, and in bronze, and in the cutting of stones for settings, and in the carving of wood, in order for him to work in all kinds of craftsmanship. And behold, I Myself have appointed with him Oholiab, the son of Ahisamach, of the tribe of Dan; and in the hearts of all who are wise at heart I have put wisdom, that they may make all that I have commanded you: the tent of meeting, and the ark of testimony, and the mercy seat upon it, and all the furniture of the tent, the table also and its utensils, and the pure gold lampstand with all its utensils, and the altar of incense, the altar of burnt offering also with all its utensils, and the laver and its stand, the woven garments as well, and the holy garments for Aaron the priest, and the garments of his sons, with which to minister as priests; the anointing oil also, and the fragrant incense for the holy place, they shall make them according to all that I have commanded you."

One of mine and my siblings' biggest pleasures have always been to always assist our father in some sort of way in ministry, it gives us some sort of value that we are also doing God's work through our father. The reality is that we were actually born to him with the different gifts we have because God knew that through our gifts and talents, he will always have someone to call upon when it comes to ministry work.

The reality is that when it comes to doing God's work, nobody has been called to do it alone because they'll easily be burnt out especially when it comes to doing the work of a team on their own, you may have received the calling and the command but the reality is that you will always need someone to help you actually make that command from God to come into fruition because there are certain things which in reality you have limited knowledge of but there could be someone else who has the very knowledge that you need to do what God called you to do.

In Exodus 31:1-11, you find God telling Moses about Bezalel and Oholiab who would be the ones to actually build the tabernacle that God gave to Moses to write down. I'm not sure about you but not many people can actually take something that's written down and create something that is perfectly what the writer intended for them to write but God gave them the knowledge and wisdom through the Holy Spirit to be able to make a perfect tabernacle that God instructed Moses to write down.

It is usually the same with me and my siblings when we do something for our father, it's usually exactly what dad wanted, sometimes we do make some mistakes of course and not do it perfectly but we have learnt to always depend on the Spirit when it comes to creating the stuff our father might need us to create for him because that's when it comes being a perfect craft. God gave my father nine children who are very creative but our creativity is always something dad has once needed or will eventually need, some of the things we know how to do we were never taught at all and the funny part is that if something is challenging for us we always find a way to figure it out at the end of the day.

One thing I've realized though is that whenever we visit a different church we see how the children of that preacher are also of very great assistance to him and how they also have the natural abilities according to his needs. That's when I then realized that by us having these gifts and talents it's because we are also called into the ministry and it's the ministry of assisting the preacher. God knew that as a preacher, you are a shepherd to many people that you need to shepherd but the reality of a shepherd, it also needs someone to help them if the sheep kraal needs fixing and people from outside are of great assistance in that department but then again if there is a young trainee shepherd there, he might be happy to find a way to fix that kraal.

Our calling is from birth because the first people to know and see the gifts that God has given us are our parents, and they utilize them in the ministry and through that, that's when God also trains us even on them so that when we grow and find ourselves needing to use them for someone else who's not our father or even for our own ministry, it has been perfected and our craft is then used for the ministry that now is beyond just our father's ministry but the ministry of the Church as a whole in the entirety of the world.

I truly encourage you to find the gift you have and if you have and once you have, find ways where you can use it in God's ministry whether it'd be for your father or maybe even for the church you currently fellowship in. God alone gives the different gifts and talents and He gives them so us as His children can use it for the Church because God knows the diversity of the Church and people always need different things to understand the gospel of Jesus because our minds are completely different from each other like the fingerprints we have, so use that gift and don't be ashamed of it, there's nothing that's insignificant in God's kingdom, everything is needed and necessary and through your gift and talent you will lead someone to Christ and he/she will have eternal life through you.

Chapter four

Prioritizing Prayer

Since I was a child and even now as an adult, each and every single day in my family we have evening prayers, everything stops and we take some time to sit together as a family and have a prayer time together. My father started this tradition, he was never taught it by anyone other than God, Himself. My father has did it and even now we can always go back and say that the only thing that kept us together through it all was the fact that we sat together to pray every night and that is something that everyone reading this book should actually know about our family, we may have been through so much but through the instruction by God and the obedience by my father of prayer each night, we were united through the Holy Spirit and I would encourage each and everyone to also try to find a way to implement this and yes, you may not have a family that believes in God but I would encourage you to always find a time in the evening where you pray over your family and if you have a sibling or parent that's also Christian, you can invite them to also join you in your prayer time.

You may not know it but prayer is one of the most important things you can do in your walk with God especially as a preacher's child because it is the only thing that can help you be able to hear the voice of God vs the voice of any of your parents, it creates a relationship with God through each and every prayer you make. You get to know who God is by yourself and He gets to reveal himself to you. Prayer is also a weapon against anything that you might face in this world because through prayer you win so many battles, even battles that you don't know you are fighting. Prayer is a formal conversation with God, that means that it is very important to be in constant conversation with God because He is the only person who sees you and is with you always, there's a beauty in the intimacy of your relationship with God when you get to literally walk and talk to Him because then, He's not only your God but also your Father, the Father that's always ready to hear any of your issues and will carry any burden for you that you might find yourself scared to share even with your preacher father, I know sometimes it does happen when you have some fear in being transparent with your family about certain things because they're Christians, there is Someone though you can depend on who is more dependable. That is your one and only Creator, YHWH.

Matthew 11:28-30

"Come to Me, all who are weary and heavy-laden, and I will give you rest. Take My yoke upon you and learn from Me, for I am gentle and humble in heart, and you will find rest for your souls. For My yoke is easy and My burden is light."

Those are the words of Jesus, it just goes to show how important it is in your own quiet time to give Him all your burdens and all your troubles because God never intended for you to do any heavy lifting and through having a life where you're in constant conversation with God, it makes it so much easier that you don't lose the intimacy with Him when you having your different prayer times through the day because that is when you can be more honest with Him through prayer.

It might sound weird but for me when I was younger, I found it so hard to learn how to pray and now I know why that was but it definitely seemed weird having a preacher's child who struggled to learn how to pray especially one who attended a multitude of services throughout his life. It was only later when God revealed to me that I had been trying to pray and sound like other people in the church whom I heard praying and I'm not sure how many can relate to that but what helped me and it may sound pretty obvious but it's the same as speaking to someone you're around most of the day, to me that my family and then once I started speaking to Him in that way, that was when I started understanding and knowing how to actually pray.

We are prone to knowing the Lord for ourselves through reading His Word, it is through that practice that may sound simple yet it is filled with so much that you can get from it that helps you in your relationship with God, that also helps you also know and learn how to pray because with the Holy Spirit, you will be able to pray scriptures and speak His Word even in your prayers because you have gotten to a different type of intimacy that cannot be taken away by anyone else and that will help you be able to know how to pray over any circumstance.

Once you've learnt how to pray, it'll be so easy to just turn it into a habit, you just simply start by remembering to pray over each and every meal you eat, it sounds quite like I'm just saying something that is rather obvious and everyone already does it but little do you know that it is so easy to forget to pray over a meal you are having or about to have simply because once you sit down, your body easily reacts to the food in from of it and just takes a bite from it and one bite leads to another and at the end of it all you have finished a meal without saying a prayer before

SEED OF A SERVANT

it. On average you eat 3 meals a day and at least 2 snacks so that means that through the simple act of praying before each time you eat, you pray 5 times a day as it is and through that it is also very easy to then do it everyday. You eat everyday and that would mean that you'll be praying everyday automatically.

Once you have got that down, you will then find it very easy to then also include God before you go to the shop, go to a meeting, go to school, speak to someone, each morning as you wake up and each night as you sleep.

Earlier in this chapter I mentioned having constant conversation with God and that can easily happen because each and every moment you find yourself thinking about something and you can use your thoughts to talk to God, He knows our thoughts. You can also speak vocally, having a conversation with Him with your tongue each chance you get, when you're walking somewhere alone, when you're in the bathroom, when you find any moment where it's just you alone with Him, that's your moment to open your mouth and speak to your Father.

James 5:16
"Therefore, confess your sins to one another, and pray for one another so that you may be healed. The effective prayer of a righteous man can accomplish much."

It might seem rather daunting when you first learn that you need to pray for other people because that means that they're trusting in your prayers to get answers/to stand with them in the prayer they're currently praying. It does seem like something big especially if you've seen your parents praying other people all through your life, that's when you might panic not knowing what to do because you are finding yourself for the very first time actually doing something that you see as "significant" when it comes to things you do in the ministry of God's church. We have a mission to pray for people, I have seen just how you can be intimidated at first because of that. However, it is important to remember to pray for people and learn how to lay hands on other people because that is what the Bible commanded us to do and in praying for other people it is especially important to remember to even pray for those who God put in our hearts to pray for, including our enemies so they can see the light.

Never forget to allow the Holy Spirit to lead you in the ways that you pray for other people because He will know how to make sure you know the words that you need to say that will help the people at the end of it all and your prayers always give courage to the people and give them hope that God is truly listening to them even if they feel like God is very far away from them.

The most important person to always pray for is your parent who is involved in the church because you are the one who gets to see everything that other people don't see and the reality is that sometimes you might be the only person in the whole world who will pray for your dad because other people won't know what can they pray for your father concerning because our parents have a very good way of making sure that they don't show everything they're going through. We may not see it but they always need someone to hold them up through prayer because God is all knowing and that means that God knows what we don't know and even how we pray for them will be led to us by the Holy Spirit.

<u>Best ways to pray for your parents in ministry</u>

- **Wisdom** - You may look at them and think they're the wisest people ever, which is actually true but let's remember that real wisdom comes from God and wisdom is not something that you get once but you have to keep on going back to get more and more. You also need to have wisdom for a particular situation like for instance there could be a situation in which they don't have any experience in how to deal with it but through getting wisdom from God they'll know exactly how to navigate through it. So pray for God to give them endless amounts of wisdom whether it could be in a situation or in a message they need to deliver to the church on a Sunday.

- **Revelation** - It is through having preached myself that I realized how much one needs true revelation from God when one is preparing a message to deliver in a church on any given Sunday. It is not as simple as finding a passage of scripture and then deciding a title and then speaking for the next 45 minutes based on the title you have, you need to have God involved through the entirety of the process so He can give you the perfect way to deliver the sermon. So our prayer plays a part in that through actually giving them the peace of mind that they need to hear what God is leading them to speak on this coming Sunday.

- **Steadfastness** - We have seen it quite a few times in the Bible and even in reality that it is so easy for a person chosen by God to fall into a snare prepared by the enemy that will in some cases end up destroying the very ministry that the preacher worked very hard to build. So our prayers can help them stay steadfast in what God has called them to and not fall for any of the temptation presented to them by the enemy.

- **Protection** - Our parents' work in the ministry is honestly quite a high risk calling because it is literally doing the one job which the enemy loathes for anyone to do because it is the work that is basically working fully against the enemy and his kingdom of darkness. There are always two kinds of dangers that they are always facing on any given day, physical danger and spiritual danger. Physical danger comes in the form of people who themselves don't like Christianity for any given reason, or who just want to sacrifice the blood of a servant of Christ to get luck from the dark side. Spiritual danger is when the enemy sends his evil minions to do the dirty work through dreams and different ways, they also try to attack the preacher who is always delivering people from the evil spirits that torment them. So our prayer is basically building a wall of fire around them to be protected from anything the enemy is trying to do to attack the preacher.

Chapter five

Unlearning the wrong kinds of teachings

In all my life I can be sure to say that I've heard more than 3000 different sermons and teachings and even though I can't remember them all, there are certain things now as an adult, were things that were either not things meant to be interpreted the way I interpreted them and I took them out of context but there were some that I can fully say that actually inaccurate with who God is.

Whenever someone stands behind a pulpit, they are there to show God to the people in some sort of way and sometimes they do have the tendency of misrepresenting to God in some sort of way to the body and at the end of the day that means other people will go home in a state of mind that is truly not what God intended for them to walk away having.

For sure, sometimes the minister can do it by mistake and it has happened quite a few times and for me I know once again from experience that when you are behind the pulpit it is possible to word something in a way that you are not intending to because of a few different reasons and people may listen to you. So that is very possible and the truth is that sometimes we do need to really pray for God to speak through us at all times in the sermons so we won't say the wrong thing at the wrong time.

Now we, people who grew up in a church are very prone to hearing something and easily believing it because as younger

Christians it is very easy to believe anything that is said by someone on the pulpit because we are taught that everything someone says behind the pulpit is straight from God. However, it is a disservice to tell someone that and not also give them a warning that there are some people in this world who take the pulpit as a pedestal to say anything they want to say and lead people astray. Somehow it has been normalized in churches, people mock God in churches more than anywhere else and it is such a serious danger to the people of God when they're being poured into by a well of dirty water. We tend to take what we were taught and walk it through in our lives and sometimes it is only through the leading of God that we do end up reading the Bible for ourselves when we realize that there are certain things that we were taught to do in our Christian walk that is not something God ever wanted us to do.

You can identify a false teaching through reading the Bible yourself while allowing the Holy Spirit to actually reveal it to you on how it is translated and what was truly meant in the passage of scripture that you are reading, if someone taught you something that cannot be found in the Bible then it is truly something that needs to be investigated through the Holy Spirit, the Bible truly has everything that you can think of.

Revelation 22:18-19

"I bear witness to everyone who hears the words of the prophecy of this book: If anyone adds to them, God will add to him the plagues which are written in this book. And if anyone takes away from the words of the book of this prophecy, God will take away his part from the tree of life and from the holy city, which are written in this book."

Deuteronomy 12:32

" Whatever I am commanding you, you shall be careful to do; you shall not add to nor take away from it."

The Bible is truly not something that you should be very careful when it comes to how you interpret it because only it is the Word truly from God that has the breath of the Holy Spirit, so that means nobody can add their own to it or take away from it according to their own liking because they're human and the power of God's word is something that we have no power over at all because God's power is the very essence of the Word of God. So it is very important to understand that we need to use the Word of God to check the validation of the different things that people are saying and even though they can use the word of God themselves, the Word of God always has context and someone who is speaking God's truth will use the very context that is the Word of God to back up what they're saying and many people can use a single verse to make anyone believe in what they're saying but the reality is that the Bible always has an endless amount of context for anything that someone will need so make sure to always read the Bible for yourself and through that you will know how to make sure you fully know when someone is using the Bible in the wrong context and then you'll know not to take anything anyone is telling you.

If you have listened to something and believed it and have been acting it out, now is the time to actually do research on it because there could be a few things you'll find out from being intentional on searching what you were living which wasn't taught to you in the right way.

Even when we find ourselves in a place where we can teach something to someone, it is vital that we ensure that what we teach is really something that is directly from God. He is the one that leads each and every thing we do. He will know how to make us know exactly what to say to that person.

I fully believe that when God speaks to an individual, He will speak to them in a language that is only understandable to that individual because considering the fact that He created us, He will know exactly how to speak to us on a multitude of different things.

The part of unlearning is rather difficult because anything you have done for a long time and believed in for a long time, your mind is hardwired to it so that means it is fully stuck in your mind and no matter what you can do, unfortunately, you can't forget. It is usually the things we were taught when we were younger, when our minds were still ready to take anything in and now that we are older, there is truly so much that is in our heads and we find it very hard to declutter our minds from all the things that are not of God, especially things that are not of God but were taught to us in His name and by someone who was supposed to be speaking under the leading of God.

Unlearning comes into play once you've been able to identify what was taught to you that is actually wrong. At first it will be so hard and in some cases you'll face a lot of opposition when it comes to the changes you've implemented in your life which were things that people know to be as "Christian" that you are no longer partaking in, I can promise you though that when it comes to you having this intimacy that you have with God, you won't find anything anyone says that will phase you or leave you confused because God, Himself, will make sure that you know you are loved and accepted by Him.

When you unlearn something, it is very important to then learn something new in the same sphere of what you just had to unlearn because through that you are not just leaving an empty void in your life. God will always show you the different way that you actually should be taking because He is your leader and your father so He will most definitely lead you to a whole new path that will lead you to an abundance in life.

Isaiah 30:20-21

"Though the Lord gave you adversity for food and suffering for drink, he will still be with you to teach you. You will see your teacher with your own eyes. Your own ears will hear him. Right behind you a voice will say, "This is the way you should go," whether to the right or to the left."

Now that you have changed, do not despise the ones who still walk in the way you used to walk in, your relationship with God is just that, your relationship with God, that means that you should allow other people to also walk their own journey with God and only if they ask you about it you share what you know and even then don't even expect for them to follow in your footsteps because people need to follow and by following God they can't follow you.

Chapter six

Having the heart of discipline

It is very easy for others to just have the assumption that us, preachers' children, are people that can not at all be disciplined when it comes to our Christian walk because "How can you reprimand and discipline the child of the boss (The pastor" that is something that I've noticed that they believe that we are very free to do anything we want and if someone tries anything with us, they'll have to deal with our dad.

That is something where in corporate it works very well, but in church there is truly no such thing because our parents are not the boss of any church, if they are truly called by God, they will know and understand that God is the real boss of the church and when it comes to God's disciplined, there is nobody at all that has a free pass to it at all, in actuality, my father and all of us are the ones who can be more prone to it than anyone else.

You might be reading this as a preacher's child and be thinking to yourself "But it's unfair, we are supposed to be treated specially" well my friend, you have got it all wrong. One of my favorite chapters in the Bible is Matthew 16 because in verses seventeen to nineteen, you see Jesus giving Simon a new name (Peter) and calling him blessed but then when you read verses twenty-one to twenty-three you see Jesus reprimanding the same Peter He blessed a few verses above. That just goes to show that with God, there is no need to fondle anyone because they're "special" it is something you need to fully understand that God disciplines because He loves you and He will even use people in the church and maybe even your own parents to discipline you for anything you are doing that is wrong because they all love you and they want you to be the best version of yourself.

Being submissive to any sort of leader's reprimand is how you set yourself for being a leader because you are understanding the fundamentals of what Godly leading looks like, it looks like putting someone first and treating them with the love and respect that you want for yourself. That means we intentionally see ourselves as imperfect people whom God is perfecting through the leadership of our parents and maybe even other church members. True humility is actually knowing your place is under the leadership of everyone in the world including the people you see as the people who you are leading.

The best person to learn humility from is your father because the term "pastor" literally means shepherd and shepherds are servants of the farmer (the owner of the sheep), which in the case of a church is God, Himself, He is the one who really runs the Church. The best way to know someone who has been truly called by God into any sort of leadership role, they're the biggest servants ever, you will see them working the hardest on anything they do. You will also see them always ready to take any correction they might get from anyone, even people who are under their own leadership. When God calls you, He calls you to be a servant and all your work is serving in humility and joy.

Another side of living a disciplined life is the side where everything is completely up to you, that is of course self discipline. In the bible you find it quite often where it speaks to being a fully disciplined person in the way you talk, act and live your life.

Chapter Seven

Asking questions is allowed

Having grown up traveling in quite a lot of different churches, it is something that I have noticed that there is always a huge amount of rules that we are to follow when we're a part of a church and each church that one goes to has their own set of rules. With Christianity being the biggest belief system in the whole world, it is not lost on us that there are an estimated 3-4 million different churches in the world and as much as there are a multitude of different denominations, that doesn't mean that each and every church is the same as another church. Each church is led by a different pastor and by that, it stands to reason that each church on its own has 1 or 2 rules which are uniquely only found in that church because each person, even Christians think in their own ways, what's fine for a different preacher won't be fine for another.

Going to churches for most of our lives we hear many different things about rules and some even go as far as to even say something is found in the bible when it's not in the Bible or if it is there is a possibility that it has been mistranslated. Somehow these rules are rules that are enforced in a way that whenever we even try to ask a question the statement we hear the most is "Of course you wouldn't know this, your father is a pastor so you don't have to follow this rule". The reality though, is that whenever we do ask a question about a rule or a statute that is placed, we just want to understand more, not to protest the rule at all. This is when we then think we are not allowed to ask any questions about anything as the ones who get an easy way around these rules being enforced upon us.

There's also the other extreme where we are expected to know each and every rule and follow it to the T, this is when the rules aren't told to us because we should already know them by heart or the other pastor may think our father has the same exact rules as he does so when we don't do what we are supposed to do or we do what we aren't supposed to do then we are rebelling because our father is also a pastor. The reality of what I've seen through my own father and through quite a few different fathers who are preachers is that some of them are the kind to not have too many rules that aren't from the Bible so things like how we dress, how we talk, how we eat, and how we live are all based on the Bible and to other people, seeing someone wearing jeans to church or a hoodie to church seems very sinful and yet for my father it is fine just as long as it is something that obviously has anything about it that's against Christianity.

Having any kind of relationship does require one to always be asking questions about that other person so they can really get to know them and also keep track with the different things they're discovering about them. Believe it or not, the more you discover about someone or something the more curious you get. It is natural for each and everyone.

I am a writer today because I found reading very interesting and I had so many questions about writing and still do have a multitude of questions when it comes to this art of writing and I wouldn't trade this gift God has given me for anything that the world can offer me.

The reality is that when you ask a multitude of questions about Christianity or the different religions doesn't mean that you are degrading the belief and faith of your parents, you are simply trying to understand everything better and you are simply widening the broadness of your headspace when it comes to the difference between what God wants you to know and do vs what anyone else wants you to know and do. God created in us the brain that has this curiosity and nothing can cure the human race from curiosity regardless of what anybody can do. When we actually tap into curiosity and there is someone who can actually help us as we wrestle with these different questions, that's when we'll find ourselves actually having a very good relationship with God.

The most heartbreaking part for any preacher's child who had questions about faith is when the people in the church and sometimes event their own parents aren't patient with them enough to actually sit with them and try to understand their perspective then next thing the child ends up leaving the faith and going in the world, the reality is that when a preacher's child leaves Christianity in most cases, it's when their questions weren't answered and they felt very unseen and unheard. Through that feeling that's when they try something different, when you have grown up believing in something and then when you have questions within you that you feel the need to ask people and the people shut you out or sometimes even crucify you saying things such as "You can't doubt God" or sometimes its "Your question is very disrespectful" the reality is that when we do conjure up the courage to ask these questions, it's after a very long time of us just trying to come to terms with them on our own. These questions don't come out of nowhere but it's questions that come to fruition because as much as we know about the Bible and God, there are still things we don't know and just because you know, it doesn't mean that everybody else should also know, God gave you that knowledge so you'll be able to patiently answer any and every questions that you have and if you don't know the answer to a question just simply say so, there's nothing with admitting to the limitation of the knowledge you have. When you give the wrong answers just because you can't admit when you don't know is actually leading someone down the wrong path and someone will be misled because you are too prideful to admit when you don't know something and the reality is that if you do admit that you don't know something, you get so much more respect from the person because you are showing them that you are only human and there are certain things that you don't know.

It is important to note that there will be times when your questions won't be answered whether by people or God, that sometimes happens and I can't tell you the reason why but what I can say is that when you get to heaven and have eternal life you will get the answers to all your questions the big, the small and even the ones you never thought to ask. These questions, for me, have been more than the ones that I have received answers to and sometimes that could be different for each person and the reality is that the answers that you need now, God will give to you and the answers that you don't need now will wait for the right time. At the end of it all it all depends on the time God set out for you to get these answers and even through whom you will get these answers.

Chapter Eight

Healing is an art

If you know the Hearthstones family quite personally you would know that my father and in turn even us, the children have been hurt by quite a few different churches of all kinds in our lifetime. From churches trying to separate us as a family to churches actually rejecting us because of our honesty and the fact that we stand for the truth and the truth we stand for is God's truth. Through this there have been many times where I have found myself in conversations with people where they have been flabbergasted by the fact that I am still Christian and even my siblings are also Christians, usually the reply I have to that is a simple "We saw God more than we saw the actions of those people against us". However, the reality is that all this should, in reality, have caused us to just turn our backs on God and go and do our own things that have nothing to do with Christianity or even the church but it was through the prayer of our parents and even their wise leadership that have kept us in the faith even through the pain of being hurt by people that are supposed to be the ones who are your Godly family.

Healing from such things is very complex and the reality is that to actually heal, one does actually need the reassuring hand of God in their life. The real thing about church hurt is that as a preacher's child, you are more prone to church hurt than anyone else because you get to see behind the scenes, you get to see your parent crying tears when they've been hurt, you get to see your parent working very hard in the church but all they get is rejection and as a preacher you are just expected to take in on the chin and move on. However, the children can't move on, the memories stay there for a very long time, it just stays there and it replays constantly and the reality is that we do find it harder to forgive the people who hurt our parents because they're the strongest people we know and when they've been hurt it does actually bother us and sometimes we even wish to get revenge on their behalf, but if the parents are parents that truly live for God, they will know how to help us as we wrestle with the idea of being hurt in such a way by people we trust the most and they will pray for us to get the heart of forgiveness towards all of these people regardless of what they have done.

The crazy part about all of this is that forgiving, as much as it's hard, is actually easy. The part that is hard is to be able to heal fully, to be able to move on from it and learn how to trust people again after another person broke your trust in the worst way possible.

It is truly hard to even open yourself up to people because you really don't know their intentions and sometimes even the people that do come to you or your family with pure intentions, you find it hard to believe because you have been so hurt by so many people that you don't know who is being real vs who is being malicious. The reality is that we can't ever fully know a person which is why our trust needs to start with God and then everyone else.

Sometimes there are people who come into your life with pure intentions but overtime their mindset changes to something else. The hard part about that is that by the time, you are hurt, you are hurt by the person whom you have fully trusted and someone who you never expected to do anything to you and the reality is that after this betrayal it'll be impossible to actually trust a person ever again. No matter how much and how long we know a person, it is very important to always remind yourself that anything can happen. The enemy can influence anybody into doing something wrong because the enemy understands that while we live in the flesh we are weak and if we surrender to the flesh it is then easy to now do something that we wouldn't have ever thought we would do.

To heal, the first thing to remember is that the person who hurt you is God's creation and God loves them more than anything and even God wants what's best for them. The same way they hurt you is the same way that you could have hurt someone else, all of us are the same and we can all hurt people especially while we are in this body. So God loves them and because God loves them it is very important for you not to hate them for what they've done.

Another thing to remember is that some people hurt other people unintentionally, something you do everyday can hurt another person very much so what is normal to them may not be normal to you at all because you are completely different from them. God created us diverse and it is a beautiful thing to be created diverse but our diversity can sometimes cause a few things to happen in our lives that hurt us or hurt other people. Being considerate of other people is always a vital part of our lives, think of someone the same way you think of yourself. That's why the Bible says "Love your neighbor as yourself". That means the same way you love yourself and treat yourself is how you should treat other people and the unfortunate part is that it happens automatically in most cases. The way you see yourself is how you will see other people, if you have a low self esteem and always find faults in yourself, you will always find faults in other people. So when you live your life just remember this one thing that you need to learn how to love yourself and fully love yourself because God loves you so much and God sees you as perfect and without faults. So other people may have hurt you unintentionally because that's how they saw themselves and what they did to you is most probably something that could have been done to them.

Whenever something has been done to you, it is important to use discernment whenever you want to talk about it. Sometimes you can want to talk about it but then when you want to talk about it, your intentions and heart isn't pure and you haven't fully healed from it. You don't need to tell people about something that has happened to you immediately, you first need to heal from it and allow God to work within you concerning that particular issue and God will help you heal it. Remember that He is the one who is the author of your life and the same as when I write fictional stories, I know where my character's story will end and I know for sure that he/she will be fully happy at the end of it, it is the same with God, He will help you heal through your very own story and He will show you how to actually be able to move on from being hurt in such a way. When you have fully healed is only when you can then speak about it but now it is not a sympathy plea but it is a testimony of what God has done to you and your family and I have seen it in my family just how much allowing God to heal us can help us to then one day be able to share the testimony of what has happened to us and we are always happy to share all the testimonies we have.

On the 7th of July 2023, it was a normal Friday, my two brothers woke up and went to work and the rest of the family carried on with the day, Fridays are the day of the week where I do the chores in the family so I cooked and after having finished cooking, I sat down on the couch, put on headphones and listened to music, by this time my two brothers were back from work. My older brother then came to the living room around 18h00 and asked my parents to pray for him because he was feeling severe chest pains and they did, he then went back to the bedroom to get a short nap before we had dinner. We had the customary evening family prayer and he was still napping and we finished and he came back to the living room just before dinner had been fully dished up. While we were eating, he didn't eat at all, he was in pain but since he was sitting next to me, I could hear him softly praying for himself that the pain can go away and that God can heal him, we then did another Hearthstones customary thing that we do on Fridays which is watch our favorite paranormal shows. He always loved these as the rest of us and was as animated as us whenever something scary would show up on the tv and we'd all scream (except for dad of course) but on that day he was just as quiet as dad was. After the paranormal show ended we all would then start slowly retiring into bed, before mom went to bed she also prayed for him one more time and told him to go to sleep and he listened. About 10 minutes after he went to bed, I also retired for the night, he would always hear me coming in and never have any reaction but on this night, he was actually startled by my entering the room and he looked at me, I stopped by the door and asked him "Are you ok bro". And he said to me "Yeah I'll be fine in the morning". I changed into my sleeping clothes and turned off the lights and went to bed, read my bible and then once I was done with my reading, I locked my phone and closed my eyes so I could go to sleep. While I was still half asleep, I heard him wake up and I thought he was going to the bathroom because he usually did go to the bathroom just before he drifted off to sleep. Somehow in a matter of 3 minutes or so, I had fallen asleep too. I was woken up by my other siblings who were still up screaming, trying to get his attention from the bathroom. I then get up and as I get out of our bedroom, I see my other brother, Felix, dragging him out of the bathroom. He dragged him to the living room and started to try performing CPR on him. At this point, my brother, Faithful, was literally gasping on a single breath every 2 or 3 minutes, we called the ambulance and they were taking too long to arrive and then my other brother, Livingstone, decided to take him to hospital on his company pickup truck. So we all go to the hospital and we stand just outside the ER and link arms and start praying for him because at the time he was on his way to hospital, he was starting to grow cold. While we're praying, the nurses came and we turned around to listen to them. I could see in their eyes that this wasn't good news and as soon as she started speaking, it was confirmed. At around 23:30 on the 7th of July my brother, Faithful, passed away at the young age of 30 years old. Tears were uncontrollable, we all had such a close bond as a family, now the one child who was in the middle of the family, who was somehow able to have a good relationship with all of us at the same time was gone, we never would have expected the pain we felt there. Even now as I write this, more than a year later, the pain of that night still lingers on everyone and now the pain we have is more like the pain of a missing piece of a puzzle that should be perfectly complete.

Losing my brother is the very essence of this chapter being named **"healing is an art"**. I never would have seen healing as an art until I had to go through the art of healing after loss, I haven't fully healed and I doubt I could ever heal from it. I know that it's an art because it takes time to heal, it can sometimes tempt you into making mistakes, it takes patience, it takes wholeness but most of all it takes doing it with God. I know it's an art because each and every book I write, I can't write a single sentence without God at all, I can't write without patience, I can't write without making mistakes here and there, I can't write when I am not whole. I am sure other artists can relate to this sentiment. This experience of loss made me appreciate each and every other thing that I experienced that hurt me but I was able to heal from because this time, I am going through something where it won't take months to heal from and it won't take years to heal from.

The biggest comfort I get is in my brother's last words "I'll be fine in the morning". Those words to me actually make sense now and it might seem confusing, it seems like he wasn't fine, it seems like God didn't answer our prayers and it doesn't make sense in finding comfort for those words. However, I find comfort in them because I understand that my brother is better than ever before, in the promised place, the most perfect place, the place without any pain, the place where he is living with Jesus, imagine staying in the same place as Jesus Himself, that is the biggest honor and for me my comfort is that I know that he was telling the truth when he said he'll be fine in the morning because the morning for him, was when he breathed his last in this world and took his first breath in heaven, there wasn't any pain, the oxygen wasn't contaminated, there wasn't any worries.

Chapter Nine

You are not raised by the church

When you grow up in front of someone, it can now seem like they had a hand in raising you and they have a right to say anything they feel like saying about who you are, what you do and how you do it. However, this is not always the case. Having grown up in quite a few different churches, I realized that there weren't many people who had a hand in raising me and were always there when I grew up. I do appreciate all those who did step in when required to discipline me, give me some advice and even take it a step further and actually pray for me.

In the previous chapter I spoke about the passing of my older brother, there is one detail I didn't write there because that detail needed to be added here. In the hospital while we didn't know what was happening with my brother, a certain woman named Mrs Mjwara just arrived about 10 minutes before Faithful was pronounced dead. Mrs Mjwara is a woman who along with her family have been a part of our lives for the past 19 years, she was there on that day and she stayed with us through the night at the hospital comforting us and occasionally making us laugh through the tears. The funny part about her is that she has been with us in so many situations, the good situations and the bad situations. Her son, Ndumiso and I recently spoke about how we literally both grew together because of the friendship of our parents. Mrs Mjwara has been pretty much like my second mother and my mother has been like Ndumiso's mother because of how close we are. She has been a woman who has truly been basically someone who raised me because she has preached some impactful sermons for me, she has said some things to me that have changed my entire thought process and even corrected me in the best ways and all in all she has shown me the love which is very close to the love my mother has for me but obviously nothing can beat the love of a mother.

My favorite part of Mrs Mjwara is that she doesn't try to force herself into being a parent to me or my siblings, other people we've encountered have always tried to do that. Some people go as far as to even try to separate us from each other because they say we hinder each other, it is truly something that we have experienced and never liked from the very beginning. The reality is that when there is a child or children of a preacher in a church that is quite big, they're always prone to being judged by their each and every move by the church members, the church members always try to discredit them in any and every single way. It is actually dishonoring the parents of a child to actually try your best to discredit the child and yet the parents know what they're doing.

It is very wrong to feel entitled to thinking that you can raise someone else's child better than them especially if they're someone who God has called into ministry, the reality is that our parents are the parents that are always strict to us and it's not bad at all, it does actually shape us to be amazing people especially in the church in the future because if it wasn't for our parents' discipline then we would be very wild especially in the church and yes there are some children who are very wild in church and the parents don't do anything about it, the best thing you can do is actually pray for the family because the family really does need prayer and God might have given you this burden so you can pray only and nothing more.

When myself and my siblings grew up in a few different churches we realized that there are certain things that we are told by other people that can contradict each other in many different ways. People's beliefs are always going to be very different from each other. God created us differently. So in a world with many voices leading us here and there, we realized that we should only listen to our parents because when the Bible says "Honor your father and mother" it ends it there and doesn't add anyone else because God gives the perfect wisdom to the ones He entrusted you to.

Chapter ten

Living your life giving God all the glory

If you know me from my previous book then you know that my main skill in writing is fictional, I enjoy creating characters in my mind, living out their lives, telling people a story, teaching people something new through the stories I tell, so when God challenged me to actually write this book, I didn't think I could ever write and get this far without chickening out because it seemed like such a daunting task especially because I never knew that I could say something of value based on my own experiences and life. God reminded me though, that I didn't give myself this gift of writing and my writing is not for my own good but for His glory to be known in the world of literature. This gave me a whole new different perspective because now that I actually think about it, God gave me this gift so that means that the diversity of this very gift that He has given me is also chosen by Him and the limitations of this gift that I have are also chosen by Him and this year He gave me this idea to write this book because of a reason only He knows and I never realized it until just now that I am not writing to be a famous writer but I am writing to show the world that my God gave me this beautiful gift of which will bring Him the glory that He deserves because He is the biggest artist ever and the art of writing originated from Him when He wrote our names on the palm of His hand and how He writes our life stories.

Everyone's life is giving God all the glory that He deserves in different ways the big and the small and God has given to us the very thing that we can use to live our lives giving God the glory He deserves. Your gift may not be preaching as your father but your life actually giving God the glory He deserves means that you are utilizing the gift you have been given to full use and there is absolutely nothing that can hold you back from that at all especially because you are not doing it on your own but with God who is leading you by the hand each and every step of the way. Living your life Giving God the glory is something to be proud of because you are walking the narrow road that is hard to walk and each step you take, you need to ensure that you are careful in it because it is very easy to stumble and the reality is that there are many eyes on you waiting for you to stumble, the biggest eye is from the devil himself because he is rooting for your downfall because through your downfall then it is God's glory having the downfall. However, he doesn't understand that God can still turn things around in your life for the better and just by you living your life in such a way where you are honest with your downfalls, you are giving God the glory because you are actually being honest to the fact that you can't do it on your own but you can do it through Christ who can actually help you be able to live your life in such a wonderful way that it brings more people to Himself just by living your life bringing Him the glory.

"As He passed by, He saw a man blind from birth. And His disciples asked Him, saying, "Rabbi, who sinned, this man or his parents, that he would be born blind?" Jesus answered, "Neither this man nor his parents sinned, but this was so that the works of God might be manifested in him. We must work

the works of Him who sent Me as long as it is day; night is coming when no one can work. While I am in the world, I am the light of the world." When He had said this, He spat on the ground, made clay of the saliva, and rubbed the clay on his eyes, and said to him, "Go, wash in the pool of Siloam" (which is translated, Sent). So he went away and washed, and came back seeing. Therefore the neighbors, and those who previously saw him as a beggar, were saying, "Is not this the one who used to sit and beg?" Others were saying, "This is he," still others were saying, "No, but he is like him." He kept saying, "I am the one." So they were saying to him, "How then were your eyes opened?" He answered, "The man who is called Jesus made clay, and rubbed my eyes, and said to me, 'Go to Siloam and wash'; so when I went away and washed, I received sight." And they said to him, "Where is He?" He *said, "I do not know."
   John 9:1-12

Imagine you being born with a defect only for God to receive His rightful glory, it sounds quite crazy doesn't it? This story has always fascinated me especially because one thing I've seen about this whole thing is that you know this man was born physically blind and yet we are all born blind, blind from knowing who God is and through Him revealing Himself to us more and more each and every day we get to see Him more and more and this man like many of us needed Jesus to save him because as much as the Bible doesn't specify how old he was but surely many people could've helped him over the years but then he only gets help from Jesus and through the act of Jesus opening his eyes, God's glory was shown. Now imagine being born just to show God's glory just with your life and you might not be blind or deaf or in any sort of way disadvantaged but the truth remains that you were born to give God the glory. It is a mission we all have and us living our lives in any other way than the way God intended for us is hindering the glory of God to be shown to the people who need to see it.

The reason behind giving God the glory is simply because there are people in your life currently or there will be people in your life who will need the person that you are to believe in God and unlike our parents who are on stage actually preaching the Word of God and try to lead the lost sheep back home, you are a normal person who happens to be their child who will live your life faithfully serving God through the different gifts God has given you and even if the gift you have might be frowned upon by the people in church but as long as God gave you that gift, use it freely because God made you like that and He is very proud of you in every single way because you are using your gift without any sort of shame to bring people to His Kingdom. Never be afraid to be loud about God in the gift you have especially in the dark world that we live in, we need more people to show the diversity that can found in Heaven and through showcasing your gift, you are actually giving people a piece of heaven and that small piece of heaven is exactly what people need sometimes and God's glory is shown.

Remember to always stay humble because you are under the authority of God and the authority of your father so everything you do, do it in humility and understand that the glory and praise go to God always!

Chapter eleven

Five main things I learnt from my father that I couldn't learn anywhere else

- **Read the bible everyday, it's your daily bread**

In 2008 my father gave me the Bible and if you've been to a church service with me you'll know that I use that same Bible even now, before he gave it to me, he marked out a huge amount of scriptures and I guess that was so I can read through them and as much as it took a very long time for me to read through all those marked scriptures, eventually I did it. That wasn't the end though, at the age of 10 I did my first attempt of reading through the bible in its entirety and my 10 year old mind was telling me "You've read many books so this will be easy" but I was very wrong, I read through Genesis and Exodus but when I got to Leviticus, that was where I got stuck because my child-mind somehow couldn't comprehend the book of Leviticus and the funny part is that my father never sat me down and told me to read the bible each and every day, I just did it out of boredom but then I quickly stopped when I was confused by Leviticus. My father did though, always read his own Bible around us and sometimes my father would actually quiz us on biblical stuff and whenever I would get a question wrong, I wanted to learn about it and if I got it right I was happy, I realized that the only way to get a majority of the answers right was to actually read the Bible myself almost like studying for an exam and little did I know this whole studying for an exam would end up building an intimacy with God that I could never have imagined and now I don't read it to know answers but I read it because I know I can't go a day without reading it.

• The skill of writing

The gift of writing is from God but the reality is that I inherited it from my father, he is one of the best writers that I have read. He is also very meticulous when he writes and me being his typer and editor, I've learnt so much that now I am also a writer and I don't imagine myself doing a different thing than using words to encourage people. My father really encouraged me and pushed me over the edge in my skill of writing and now I know that my writing is something that I can always use for the good and now I've also learnt to be more meticulous in my writing as he is and just the different styles of writing I've showcased, all of them I've spoken to with my father and he has given me advice and showed me the right path and allowed me to be myself at the end of the day.

• Humility

If you've met my father you would know that he is wise, has knowledge of so many different things, good with languages, good at singing, good at preaching, and a good father. However, he is very humble and other people see all those skills in him and yet he won't be prideful in them and I guess it's because he understands that God gave it all to him and God can take it away. My father is very fast in lifting others up and sometimes I get surprised when I meet one of dad's contacts somewhere and they know that I am also a writer and I realize that he talks about me a lot because he is proud of me but also the fact that he does enjoy talking about other people and giving them the honor they deserve and that really showed me to also be humble and be ready to lift other people up.

• Family comes first always!

There have been many times where people have tried to separate our family from each other in so many different ways, they have hurt us in so many ways. My family has faces so much troubles and it all could've been easy for my father to do something that could hurt us but through it all, I never had to ever doubt the fact that my father, Ps O Hearthstones loves us dearly and would never trade us for anything and my father always put us first and protected us from any harm the people tried to bring to us and now as I write this, at home with my family I always make sure they know that they always come first and anyone with malicious plans against our family will fail because I love them too much and I know the love we have for each other is mutual.

- **The necessity of prayer**

In my family we pray each and every night together, on good days and bad days, you will find us sitting somewhere together and having the family prayer time. I remember after my older brother passed away, the first thing we did after we got home even though it was after 2am was for us to pray even in the midst of tears. My father however, never just prayed with us, there have been many times when I would walk into their bedroom and find him praying. Sometimes when I see him walking whether in the yard or outside the yard, I would see his lips moving. When we faced a small spiritual warfare situation, my father taught us all in the family about spiritual warfare and how to fight it. There are so many more things about prayer I learnt about him and I have such a wonderful prayer life because I watch him and see what I need to do.

There are so many more things I can list that I've learnt from him because he has shown me so much but this lists out just the things that I believe you will also learn about this man who accepted a calling from God and thus made me and my eight siblings Seeds of a servant.

Epilogue

Would I live this life again with all the good and the bad? It's a big yes because throughout this book I shared good moments as much as bad moments and the reality is that through it all, I've never had a day when I never smiled or laughed at something.

Being born into a life surrounded by ministry is the biggest gift ever. I love being in the midst of it all and I can truly say from the depths of my heart that I love this life and I would never trade it for anything.

My message to other PKs as they're affectionately known, my friends we didn't have a choice of who we would call mom and dad and the reality is that each and every parent that we could've chosen has their own list of good you'll get from them and the bad from them. The choice comes when it comes to giving God your life in its entirety, yes I know, the church is very flawed and filled with hypocrites, yes the church will most probably hurt you but the reality is that this church can hurt everyone and you being hurt by the church means that you are just living in this flawed world that is filled with so much wrong in it. So in it all remember that you serve a perfect master, Jesus Christ who lived in this imperfect world for you and died for you. Continue in serving your parents and continue in being unashamed in who you are because God gave you the best seats of the game, the front row seats of His work in the world.

About the author...

Khethizwi Heavenlygift Hearthstones is the birth name of the author known as Heavenlygift Hearthstones originally from Ermelo, Mpumalanga currently resides in Howick, KwaZulu Natal. He found his love for words by reading books he would find everywhere, he had a plethora of books in school and at home and he took every opportunity to read them as much as he could. In 2020, he was reading "A Hiding Place" when he got inspired to turn one of the stories he's had in his mind into a book, he wrote it and it went very well and then he also wrote "Hate in the Dark" in 2021 which was the first book he published on the 8th of January 2024.

His love for words transcends to poetry, loving the rhythm one needs to perform poetry while keeping a rhyme scheme.

He also loves and analyzes lyrics of songs and always finds songwriting very fascinating.

His walk with God and love for God is easy to see in all his written work through the things he wrestles with and the things God reveals to him in his walk with Christ.

Don't miss out!

Visit the website below and you can sign up to receive emails whenever Heavenlygift Hearthstones publishes a new book. There's no charge and no obligation.

https://books2read.com/r/B-A-WTNCB-TJIAF

BOOKS2READ

Connecting independent readers to independent writers.

Also by Heavenlygift Hearthstones

Hate in the dark
Seed of a Servant

About the Author

Heavenlygift Hearthstones is an author who released his first book at 23 years old, he is from South Africa, writes Christian fiction stories and devotionals

www.ingramcontent.com/pod-product-compliance
Ingram Content Group UK Ltd.
Pitfield, Milton Keynes, MK11 3LW, UK
UKHW041847141224
452457UK00013B/747

9 798224 185153